STOP, LOOK, LISTEN

Animals

AGE 5–7

SPRING TERM 1999
Tuesdays 9.45–10.00 Repeated Fridays 9.45–10.00

1 **The Wren** *12 Jan & 15 Jan* 8370638 & 8201554
2 **Biswas the Bull** *19 Jan & 22 Jan* 8036242 & 8047358
3 **Anancy the Spider** *26 Jan & 29 Jan* 8872046 & 8703962
4 **The Cat** *2 Feb & 5 Feb* 1201821 & 1149037
5 **The Laidly Worm** *9 Feb & 12 Feb* 1047625 & 1978541

resources

Teachers' Guide
Cross-curricular work on animals, maps and stories from the programmes. **£3.95**

Activity Book
The differentiated, photocopiable activity pages in this book allow children to explore the geographical, scientific and environmental aspects of each animal's story, and provide some enjoyable activities for work on English. **£6.95**

Story Book
This 40-page hardback book contains each animal's story, beautifully illustrated to complement the television animations, and retold in simple language appropriate for young children. **£9.95**

Poster
The five animals from the programmes appear in this clear and colourful poster, which features artwork from the Story Book. 59 x 84 cm. **£3.99***

Video
5 x 15-minute programmes. **£14.99***

STOP, LOOK, LISTEN

Streetwise

AGE 5–7

SPRING TERM 1999
Tuesdays 9.45–10.00 Repeated Fridays 9.45–10.00

1 **My Street**
   23 Feb & 26 Feb 1549033 & 1487249
2 **Water for Life**
   2 Mar & 5 Mar 8147918 & 8078834
3 **Bikes, Buses and Cars**
   9 Mar & 12 Mar 8976422 & 8814638
4 **Going to the Shops**
   16 Mar & 19 Mar 8649326 & 8570242
5 **Why We Need Trees**
   23 Mar & 26 Mar 8478830 & 8316046

resources

Teachers' Guide £3.95

Resource Pack
Our Street – Our World
An everyday street scene in the UK is related to global environmental and developmental issues through linked visual material from India. Contains ★ teachers' booklet ★ colour frieze ★ four photocopiable black-and-white drawings ★ eight full-colour postcards. Published by WWF and PCET. **£17.95***

Video
5 x 15-minute programmes. **£14.99***

Topi

NAME

NAME AND ADDRESS OF SCHOOL

POSTCODE:

TELEPHONE:

ACCOUNT NUMBER IF KNOWN

Credit Card Details

Cross one: ☐ Visa   ☐ Mastercard   ☐ Delta   ☐ Switch

Card number: ☐☐☐☐ ☐☐☐☐ ☐☐☐☐ ☐☐☐☐

Valid from: Month ☐☐ Year ☐☐   Expiry date: Month ☐☐ Year ☐☐

Issue number (Switch): ☐☐   Amount of payment: £ ☐☐☐ pence ☐☐

Cardholder's Name (as on card):
Postal Address:

Postcode:

I authorise Channel 4 Schools to charge my account with the total amount of my order. Orders will be fulfilled where possible according to the availability dates stated in this order form. Availability dates refer to 1998 except where otherwise stated.

Cardholder's signature:

	AVAILABILITY	IPC	PRICE	QUANTITY	TOTAL
THE SENSATIONS					
The Sensations Teachers' Guide	Aug	217390	£3.95		
The Sensations Activity Book	Dec	216958	£6.95		
The Sensations Video	Nov	217056	£14.99*		
THE ARTS CART					
The Arts Cart Teachers' Guide	Aug	217981	£3.95		
The Arts Cart Video	Jan 99	217205	£14.99*		
THE LUNCH BUNCH					
The Lunch Bunch Teachers' Guide	Aug	187083	£3.95		
The Lunch Bunch Activity Book	Aug	217342	£6.95		
The Lunch Bunch Video	Aug	187109	£14.99*		
Maths & Food Maths Activity Book	Aug	219466	£6.95		

All prices marked * include VAT

	AVAILABILITY	IPC	PRICE	QUANTITY	TOTAL
ANIMATED BIBLE STORIES					
Animated Bible Stories Teachers' Guide	Aug	187013	£3.95		
Animated Bible Stories Activity Book	Aug	224660	£6.95		
Animated Bible Stories Video	Aug	190463	£14.99*		
FAMOUS PEOPLE					
Famous People Teachers' Guide	Aug	217581	£3.95		
Famous People Activity Book	Aug	217982	£6.95		
Story Book: George Stephenson	Aug	217206	£5.95		
Story Book: Grace Darling	Aug	217583	£5.95		
Story Book: Alexander Graham Bell	Aug	217343	£5.95		
Story Book: Mary Seacole	Aug	217983	£5.95		
Story Book: Neil Armstrong	Aug	217585	£5.95		
Story Book: Boudica	Aug	220594	£5.95		
Story Book: Leonardo da Vinci	Aug	219786	£5.95		
Story Book: Gandhi	Aug	220595	£5.95		
Story Book: Cleopatra	Aug	165725	£5.95		
Story Book: Guy Fawkes	Aug	210746	£5.95		
Famous People Video	Nov	217365	£14.99*		
MUSIC, MAGIC AND MYSTERY					
Music, Magic and Mystery Teachers' Guide	Aug	187058	£3.95		
Music, Magic and Mystery Activity Book	Aug	217586	£6.95		
Music, Magic and Mystery Story Book	Aug	164566	£9.95		
Music, Magic and Mystery Video	Aug	187094	£14.99*		
ANIMALS					
Animals Teachers' Guide	Aug	186401	£3.95		
Animals Activity Book	Aug	217985	£6.95		
Animals Story Book	Aug	164640	£9.95		
Animals Poster	Aug	217787	£3.99*		
Animals Video	Aug	187821	£14.99*		
STREETWISE					
Streetwise Teachers' Guide	Aug	187028	£3.95		
Our Street – Our World Resource Pack	Aug	187108	£17.95*		
Streetwise Video	Aug	187112	£14.99*		
STORIES OF FAITH					
Stories Of Faith Teachers' Guide	Aug	186411	£3.95		
Stories of Faith Story Book	Aug	220213	£4.95		
Maths & Festivals Activity Book	Aug	219465	£6.95		
PEOPLE WHO HELP US					
People Who Help Us Activity Book	Aug	220222	£6.95		
People Who Help Us Video	Aug	217588	£14.99*		
PLACES AND JOURNEYS					
Places and Journeys Activity Book	Aug	219209	£6.95		

All prices marked * include VAT   Total

Channel 4 Schools
PO Box 100
Warwick
CV34 6TZ

Tel 01926 436444
Fax 01926 436446

Email sales@schools.channel4.co.uk

Please send a cheque made payable to Channel 4 Schools.
Postage and packing are **free**.

STOP, LOOK, LISTEN

AGE 5–7

Stories of Faith

SUMMER TERM 1999
Tuesdays 9.45–10.00   Repeated Fridays 9.45–10.00

1 **Judaism** Joseph and his Brothers
  20 Apr & 23 Apr   7170339 & 7001255
2 **Christianity** The Good Samaritan
  27 Apr & 30 Apr   7909843 & 7847059
3 **Islam** The Journey to Medina
  11 May & 14 May   5620237 & 5551153
4 **Christianity** Zacchaeus the Tax Collector and Jesus
  18 May & 21 May   5459741 & 5397957
5 **Sikhism** The Guru and the Water Carrier
  25 May & 28 May   5295545 & 5126461

resources

Teachers' Guide
Offers differentiated photocopiable materials and suggestions to enable children to explore the spiritual, moral and religious themes of this unit. **£3.95**

Story Book
This softback book, beautifully illustrated in full colour, tells all five stories from the series, in an accessible style for adults to read to and share with children. **£4.95**

Maths Activity Book
Maths & Festivals
36 pages of photocopiable activity sheets and teachers' notes. **£6.95**

STOP, LOOK, LISTEN

AGE 5–7

People Who Help Us

AUTUMN TERM 1998
● Night-time
Tuesday 1 Dec 04.00–05.15   7774997

1 **Police Officer**
2 **Firefighter**
3 **Postal Officer**
4 **Refuse Collector**
5 **Rescuer**

resources

Activity Book
This 44-page book extends children's understanding of the work of 'people who help us' both now and in the past. Includes differentiated, photocopiable activity sheets to support each programme. **£6.95**

Video
5 x 15-minute programmes. **£14.99***

STOP, LOOK, LISTEN

AGE 5–7

Places and Journeys

SPRING TERM 1999
● Night-time
Tuesday 2 Mar 04.00–05.15   1293376

1 **Building a House**
2 **Water**
3 **From Farm to Factory**
4 **Markets**
5 **Getting There: Routes and transport**

resources

Activity Book
44 pages of photocopiable activity sheets to support each of the five programmes. **£6.95**

Topics
for 4–7 year olds
Transmissions and Resources

Stop, Look, Listen
The Sensations, The Arts Cart, The Lunch Bunch, Animated Bible Stories: The Life of Jesus, Famous People, Music, Magic and Mystery, Animals, Streetwise, Stories of Faith, People Who Help Us, Places and Journeys

---

STOP, LOOK, LISTEN

 AGE 4–6

The Sensations

AUTUMN TERM 1998
Mondays 10.50–11.00 Repeated Wednesdays 10.50–11.00
⌕ SUBTITLES

1. **Seeing**
   21 Sep & 23 Sep   3666624 & 3537168
2. **Hearing**
   28 Sep & 30 Sep   3402428 & 3366672
3. **Smelling**
   5 Oct & 7 Oct   5778308 & 5632552
4. **Tasting**
   12 Oct & 14 Oct   5507812 & 5478356
5. **Touching**
   19 Oct & 21 Oct   5343616 & 5207860

resources

Teachers' Guide £3.95

Activity Book
Fun ways for young children to investigate the world around them and increase their awareness of the senses. Includes photocopiable activity sheets.
£6.95

Video
5 x 10-minute programmes. £14.99*

STOP, LOOK, LISTEN

 AGE 4–6

The Arts Cart

AUTUMN TERM 1998
Mondays 10.50–11.00
Repeated Wednesdays 10.50–11.00
⌕ SUBTITLES

1. **Homes**
   2 Nov & 4 Nov   6901685 & 6945029
2. **Bodies**
   9 Nov & 11 Nov   6747489 & 6601633
3. **Animals**
   16 Nov & 18 Nov   6576993 & 6447437
4. **Friends**
   23 Nov & 25 Nov   6249897 & 6276941
5. **Water**
   30 Nov & 2 Dec   6078301 & 9426444

STOP, LOOK, LISTEN

 AGE 4–6

The Lunch Bunch

SPRING TERM 1999
Mondays 10.50–11.00
Repeated Wednesdays 10.50–11.00
⌕ SUBTITLES

1. **Food, Fun and Facts**
   11 Jan & 13 Jan   2799695 & 2660139
2. **Bread and Cereals**
   18 Jan & 20 Jan   2535499 & 2499643
3. **Fruit and Vegetables**
   25 Jan & 27 Jan   2364903 & 2235447
4. **Milk and Dairy Products**
   1 Feb & 3 Feb   3933178 & 3960222
5. **Festivals**
   8 Feb & 10 Feb   3762682 & 3633126

resources

Teachers' Guide £3.95

Activity Book
Ideas and guidance for exciting activities based around the topic of food.
£6.95

Video
5 x 10-minute programmes. £14.99*

Maths Activity Book
Maths & Food
For 5–7 year olds. 36 pages of photocopiable activity sheets and teachers' notes. £6.95

---

resources

Teachers' Guide
Stimulating ways to develop the themes of the programmes in the classroom. Includes
★ notes on the programmes ★ new ideas
★ suggestions for activities. £3.95

Video
5 x 10-minute programmes. £14.99*

STOP, LOOK, LISTEN

AGE 4–6

Animated Bible Stories: The Life of Jesus

SPRING TERM 1999
Mondays 10.50–11.00
Repeated Wednesdays 10.50–11.00
SUBTITLES

1 **The First Christmas**
   22 Feb & 24 Feb   3337990 & 3208434

2 **Jesus the Storyteller**
   1 Mar & 3 Mar   8294401 & 8238845

3 **Jesus the Miracle-Worker**
   8 Mar & 10 Mar   8030205 & 8901749

4 **Jesus the Healer**
   15 Mar & 17 Mar   8876009 & 8730253

5 **The First Easter**
   22 Mar & 24 Mar   8532613 & 8576057

resources

Teachers' Guide   £3.95

Activity Book   £6.95

Video
5 x 10-minute programmes.   £14.99*

STOP, LOOK, LISTEN

AGE 5–7

Music, Magic and Mystery

AUTUMN TERM 1998
Tuesdays 9.45–10.00 Repeated Fridays 9.45–10.00

1 **How Music Came to Earth**
   3 Nov & 6 Nov   8921048 & 8864709

2 **The Nightingale**
   10 Nov & 13 Nov   8687652 & 8525868

3 **Kelele and the Musical Cow**
   17 Nov & 20 Nov   8423456 & 8354372

4 **Finbar's Tale**
   24 Nov & 27 Nov   8252960 & 8190176

5 **The Ruby Prince**
   1 Dec & 4 Dec   3852371 & 3863487

resources

Teachers' Guide
Activities designed to stimulate children's language development in the contexts of music and English.   £3.95

Activity Book
Differentiated photocopiable activity sheets allowing children to explore language and music.   £6.95

Story Book
Using the original graphics from the programmes, the five stories of **Music, Magic and Mystery** are reproduced in this colourful hardback book. They are told in simple language appropriate for young children.   £9.95

Video
5 x 15-minute programmes.   £14.99*

STOP, LOOK, LISTEN

AGE 5–7

Famous People

AUTUMN TERM 1998
Tuesdays 9.45–10.00 Repeated Fridays 9.45-10.00

1 **George Stephenson – Steaming Away**
   22 Sep & 25 Sep   9538025 & 9469941

2 **Grace Darling – To The Rescue**
   29 Sep & 2 Oct   9374829 & 1582579

3 **Alexander Graham Bell – Ringing The Changes**
   6 Oct & 9 Oct   1480167 & 1311083

4 **Mary Seacole – Battling To Save Lives**
   13 Oct & 16 Oct   1146771 & 1157887

5 **Neil Armstrong – Man on the Moon**
   20 Oct & 23 Oct   1982575 & 1813491

resources

Teachers' Guide
Background information on the people featured in the programmes, and ideas for classroom activities centred around the programmes.   £3.95

Activity Book
Contains photocopiable activity sheets and accompanying teachers' notes, giving children opportunities to consolidate and advance their understanding of human history.   £6.95

Story Books
Ten full-colour 24-page information books.
George Stephenson   £5.95
Grace Darling   £5.95
Alexander Graham Bell   £5.95
Mary Seacole   £5.95
Neil Armstrong   £5.95
Boudica   £5.95
Leonardo da Vinci   £5.95
Gandhi   £5.95
Cleopatra   £5.95
Guy Fawkes   £5.95

Video
5 x 15-minute programmes.   £14.99*

Introduction

Stop, Look, Listen is Channel 4 Schools' popular topic-based series for early years. This term we are offering five programmes on **Animals**.

Since time immemorial, people of different cultures have told each other myths, stories and fables about animals. In this series five stories have been animated in a rich variety of textures and styles, and re-told to engage the viewer's imagination. Produced by Moving Still for Channel 4 Schools, **Animals** blends animation with live-action footage of animals in their natural habitat. In each programme the storyteller is the Sphinx, who uses a magic laptop computer to transport the viewer to the place, country and culture of the animal subject of the story.

The story-telling provides great opportunities for creative language development work. The factual element of the programmes will stimulate interest in geography, science, history and environmental issues.

Channel 4 Schools endeavours to work closely both with and for schools. Please help us to make the service as effective as possible by fowarding your comments about this year's series of **Stop, Look, Listen** to the address below. We would also welcome examples of children's work as a result of watching the programmes. Please send any correspondence to:

Peter Logue
Education Officer
Channel 4 Schools
PO Box 100
Warwick
CV34 6TZ

contents

Using the unit	2
Additional resources	3
Programme 1	
The Wren: The king of the birds	4
How my life began – Activity sheet 1	5
Name the birds – Activity sheet 2	6
Programme 2	
Biswas the Bull	7
Help Biswas find his way home – Activity sheet 3	8
At work – Activity sheet 4	9
Programme 3	
Anancy the Spider	10
Spider spills the wisdom – Activity sheet 5	11
Number rhyme – Activity sheet 6	12
Programme 4	
The Cat	13
Cat wants to sit by the fire – Activity sheet 7	14
Friends and foes – Activity sheet 8	15
Programme 5	
The Laidly Worm	16
Make a stained-glass window – Activity sheet 9	17
Then and now – Activity sheet 10	18
What are the animals looking for? – Activity sheet 11	19
Riddle – Activity sheet 12	20
Credits	Inside back cover
Notice board	Insert
Transmission details	Insert

Subtitles
This **Channel 4 Schools** series is subtitled on Teletext.

Using the unit
Animals

Stories and storytelling from animal folk tales around the world lie at the heart of this series. Drawing on a mixture of animation styles and live-action footage of animals in their natural habitat, the programmes also explore the interaction between animals and man.

Much information about animals is given in the series: animals of today and long ago, farm animals, tame and wild animals, creatures of land, sea and air, their habits and habitats.

The Sphinx, who is 'older than you can believe, wiser than you can understand', is the storyteller, and in the cartoon opening she calls up the story on a laptop computer, combining an ancient image with a modern one.

The animal in each story is introduced and the Sphinx tells a story which explains the animal's origins, a story which will tell him 'who he is and where he comes from': the essence of a folk tale. First, however, 'a story is always more interesting if you know something about it', so we are transported across land and sea to the location and the time in which the story is set.

The story is told as an animation, and finally we are returned to the cartoon character who summarises key points in the programme, completing the three different styles of presentation.

The follow-up activities extend and develop the ideas presented in the programme, giving opportunities for work at different levels on maps, animals and, of course, stories. The first worksheet on each programme suggests ways of telling a story, the second deals with the factual content of the programme, and the last two worksheets link all five programmes together.

Because the folk tale explains and teaches and is by its nature cross-curricular, it is an ideal vehicle for delivering topic work in Key Stage 1 as illustrated in the topic web below.

ENGLISH
- retelling a story in different ways – pictures, storyboard, animation, shadow puppets, drama, games
- telling a story from different points of view
- appreciation of dialect
- reading other animal stories/poems
- writing stories, poems, play scripts, newspaper articles

SCIENCE
- floating/sinking
- flight
- shadows, reflections
- knowledge of animals – wild and tame
- minibeasts, birds and their habitats

MATHS
- sorting, classifying, counting, measuring
- shape and space, positional words
- making a board game

PSHE/RE/CITIZENSHIP (in NI, EMU/CH)
- stories from different lands
- the role of animals in different countries
- different ideas of God
- co-operation, sharing, caring and honesty

GEOGRAPHY
- map work (local)
- locating countries on world map – Ireland, India, Caribbean, Egypt, England
- directional words
- compass points – north, south, east and west

PE
- moving and stopping on a signal
- spacing, forwards, backwards and sideways
- hopping, walking, running, jumping – hands and feet
- reflecting animal movements – quick/jerky, slow/swaying, small/fluttering, crawling, slinking, plodding and galloping

MUSIC
- tapping rhymes and rhythms
- percussion
- animal movements
- graphic score
- animal sounds
- songs about birds/animals

ART AND DESIGN
- drawing, painting, wall murals, 3D work, model making, glider making, puppet making

HISTORY
- stories of long ago
- simple timeline
- how early man tamed the animals
- early dwellings

ANIMALS

Additional resources
Animals

General

Hughes, Ted, *How the Whale Became and Other Stories*, Faber and Faber

Baumgartner, Barbara, and Moffat, Judith, *Crocodile Crocodile – Stories told around the World*, Dorling Kindersley

Mayo, Margaret, and Ray, Jane, *Orchard Book of Magical Tales*, Orchard Books

Burnie, David, and Gamlim, Linda, *First Encyclopaedia of Animals,* Kingfisher Books

Ganeri, Anita, *Maps and Map Making*, (facts, things to make and activities), Watts Books

Taylor, Barbara, Young Discoveries series – *Maps and Mapping*, (geography facts), Kingfisher

Grey et al, *Animals in Danger*, World International

Woodward, Kate, *How do animals talk?*, Usborne

The Wren: The king of the birds

Althea, *Life Cycle Birds*, Longman

Thompson, Ruth, *What's What? – BIRDS* – a flap book, Watt Books

Burton, Jane, and Taylor, Kim, *EGG – a photographic story of hatching*, Dorling Kindersley

Woodward, Kate, *How Does a Bird Fly?* – Starting Point Science, Usborne

Taylor, Barbara, *Air and Flight* – Simple Science, Kingfisher

Walpole, Brenda, *Air* – Fun with Science, Kingfisher

Ward, Alan, *Flight and Floating* – Pocket Scientist, Usborne

Carroll, Yvonne, *Irish Legends for Children*, Gill and Macmillan

Wild Life Ltd, *Fact File*, Wildlife Ltd

Biswas the Bull

Bailey, Donna, *We live in India – My World Series*, Macmillan

Das, Prodeepta, *Inside India*, Franklin Watts

Wood, Jenny, *Our Culture* series (Hindu, Buddhist, Muslim, Sikh, Jewish, Rastafarian), Franklin Watts

Althea, *Farm Animals*, Collins/Dinosaur

Grey et al, *Food and Farming* – a teachers' resource pack, Dewhurst

Anancy the Spider

Flint, David, *On the Map – Caribbean*, Simon and Schuster

Agard, John, and Nichols, Grace (eds.), *A Caribbean Dozen – Poems from Caribbean Poets*, Walker Books

Gunning, Monica, *Not a Copper Penny in me House*, Pan-Macmillan

Markanlall, David, P, Brer *Anansi's Joy Ride and Other Stories*, Blackie

Savage, Stephen, *Observing Nature – SPIDER,* Wayland

The Cat

Struan, Reid, *My Museum* – Ancient Egypt, Belitha Press

Flint, David, *On the Map* – Egypt, Simon and Schuster

Cole, Joanna, and Millar, Margaret, *My New Kitten*, Morrow Junior Books

Petty, K., *First Pets – Cats,* Franklin Watts

Dodd, Lynley, *Slinky Malinky*, Picture Puffin

Dodd, Lynley, *Slinky Malinky – Open the Door,* Picture Puffin

The Laidly Worm

Curtis, Neil, *Discovering Snakes and Lizards*, Wayland

Oram, Sandie (ed.), *Macdonald First Library – Snakes and Lizards,* Macdonald Educational

Aston, Oliver, *Lizards*, Basil Blackwell/Oxford

Robson, Pam, *Topic Books – Castles*, Wayland

Stainer, Tom, and Sutton, Harry, *Cathedrals*, BBC, Zig Zag

Useful addresses to contact

Oxfam: Education Department, 274 Banbury Road, Oxford OX2 7DX

RSPB: The Lodge, Sandy, Bedfordshire SG19 2DL

RSPCA: Education Department, Causeway, Horsham, Sussex RH12 1HG

National Farmers Union: Farming Information Centre, Agriculture House, Knightsbridge, London SW1X 7NJ

National Dairy Council, 7–9 Princes Street, London W1M 0AP

The National Trust, 36 Queen Anne's Gate, London SW1H 9AS

The Countryside Commission, 19–23 Albert Road, Manchester M19 2EQ

The National Book League, Book House, 45 East Hill, London SW18 2QZ

PROGRAMME 1

The Wren: The king of the birds
A story from Ireland

Learning outcomes

As a result of the programme children should have had experiences which enable them to:

- listen to, enjoy and retell the story
- recognise that there are differences between a folk tale and a 'true' story
- understand what a map is and be able to draw or make a simple plan
- recognise a variety of birds and learn something about their habitats
- understand something about flight

Programme outline

This first programme in the series introduces us to the Sphinx, who tells the story of how the wren tricked the eagle to become king of the birds. The story is set in Ireland and illustrates the proverb 'Huna bhfuil tu laidir caitfhidh tu bheith glic' – 'If you are not strong you have to be clever'. We travel over the physical features of the landscape, learn something about birds – the wren in particular – and discover that this is a story of long ago.

Key vocabulary

strong/strongest, fast/fastest, high/higher/highest, weather vane, direction, distance, competition, referee

Before the programme

- Talk to the children about the idea that *might* is not always *right*.
- Make a plan of the classroom and help the children to map where they sit.
- Talk to the children about a 'bird's-eye view' and do some work on a map or plan of the school area.
- Locate Ireland on a globe or map of the world.
- Look at some playground birds and identify them.
- Look at pictures of other birds, especially the eagle, owl and wren if they were not found in the local environment.

Whilst watching

Programmes are best viewed initially without interruption. However, the pause/stop/start facility on VHS may be used to creative advantage, for example to draw children's attention to aerial views and the direction in which the Sphinx travels to locate the story. Children can be helped to differentiate between live-action sequences and animations.

Follow-up activities

▶ Discuss old and new stories.

▶ Hot-seat Eagle to talk about his failure and Wren's trickery.

▶ Retell the story from the point of view of Eagle.

▶ What did the other birds think of Eagle? Divide the children into groups of four (Starlings, Sparrows, Seagulls and Bluetits) to discuss their feelings about Eagle's pride.

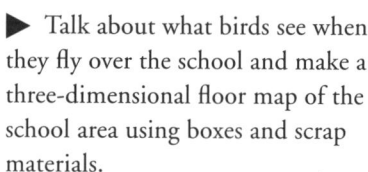

▶ Talk about what birds see when they fly over the school and make a three-dimensional floor map of the school area using boxes and scrap materials.

▶ Observe playground birds and make a graph of how many of each kind can be seen.

▶ Make a bird cake and put up a winter bird table. The second worksheet 'Name the birds' is a reinforcement of the children's observations.

▶ Find out what different birds eat.

▶ Make a bird mobile.

▶ Read the story of Icarus, and talk about early attempts at flight.

▶ Make paper gliders, experiment to see which flies highest/farthest and record the results.

▶ Talk about animation in the context of the programme and explain that a great number of individual drawings are needed to make movement.

▶ Use the worksheet 'How my life began' as a very simple timeline to tell the story of the bird's development from egg to adult bird.

How my life began

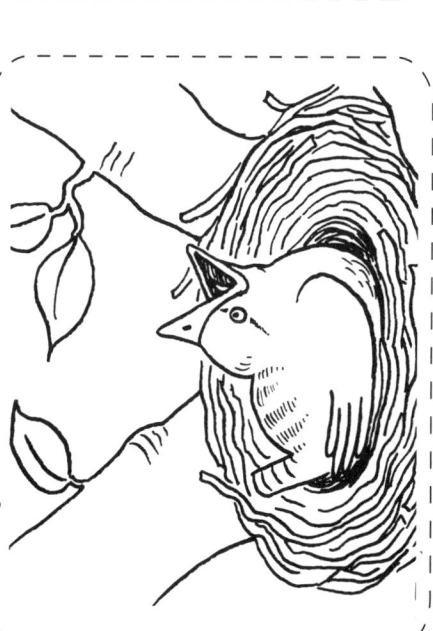

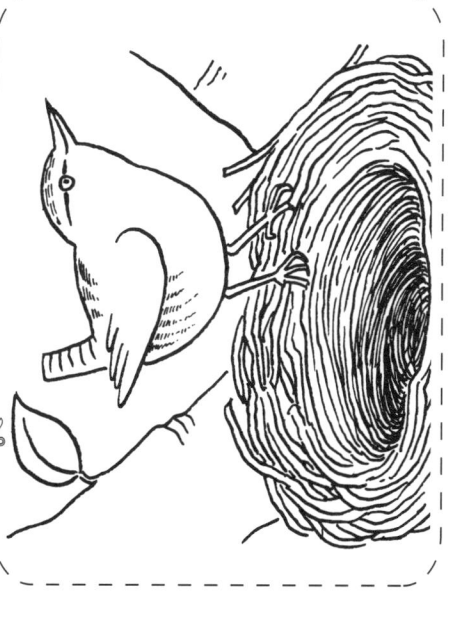

Colour and cut out the pictures.
Put them in the right order to tell a story.

Name the birds

bluetit seagull thrush sparrow robin blackbird

Biswas the Bull A story from India

Learning outcomes

As a result of the programme children should have had experiences which enable them to:

- begin to understand that stories which explain who we are, and where we come from, are told in every land
- learn something about India and appreciate some differences in cultures
- know that different animals live in different climates and countries
- understand that Biswas' journey can be described in picture form as a map
- understand that man's use of cattle has developed through the ages

Programme outline

The story tells of how Biswas, the Indian Humpbacked Bull, leaves the farm and makes a journey through the countryside to discover who he is. He encounters and is rebuffed by water buffalo and elephants, and only when he recognises the shadows of two adult humpbacked bulls coming towards him does he know his identity.

In the course of the programme we learn how man has tamed and kept cattle and how they are revered in India today. We take a look at a wide variety of wild and dangerous animals.

Key vocabulary

journey, discover, map, wild, tame, dangerous, over, under, through, across, around

Before the programme

- Locate India on a map of the world.
- Point out north, south, east and west.
- Discuss how animals are used in different countries.
- Show pictures of a humpbacked bull and explain how cattle are revered in India.
- Look at some shadows in the playground.

Whilst watching

Pause the programme to observe the maps of the countries over which the Sphinx travels and to note that she is going east for this story. Look at shadows and the position of the sun.

Follow-up activities

▶ Dramatise the story, emphasising the physical features of the landscape.

▶ Tell the story from different points of view: Biswas, the farmer, the water buffalo or the elephants.

▶ Make a simple timeline of what children do at different times of the day and note the changing position of the sun.

▶ Look at a map of the world and locate India in relation to the UK. Show where there are high mountains and great rivers.

▶ Find out about Indian culture and customs. If your school is not in a multicultural community, try to find out about different cultures. Invite someone (perhaps a parent) from an Indian or Asian community to talk to the class about his/her culture and lifestyle.

▶ Research cattle in different lands and through the ages.

▶ Find out all you can about Indian humpbacked bulls before tackling the worksheet 'At work'.

▶ Teach positional words, for example 'over', 'under', 'above', 'through', 'across', 'around'.

▶ Use the worksheet 'Help Biswas find his way home' to retrace Biswas' journey as a board game. Stick the photocopied sheet onto a card, cut out and make spinner dice and Biswas markers.

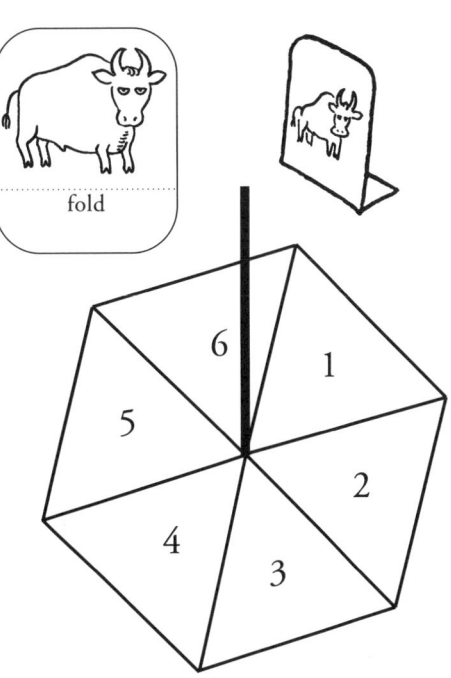

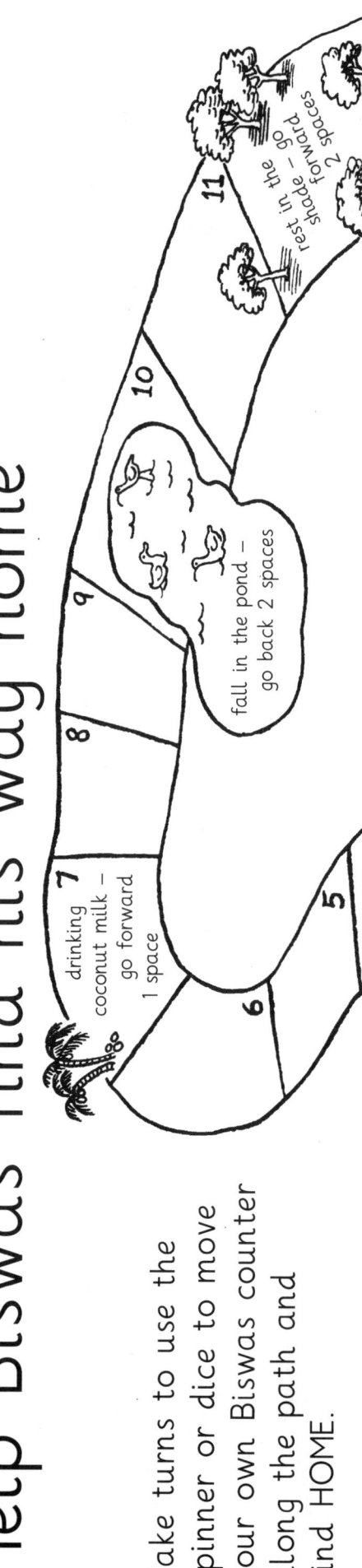

Help Biswas find his way home

Take turns to use the spinner or dice to move your own Biswas counter along the path and find HOME.

ACTIVITY SHEET 4

At work

These Indian humpbacked bulls are at work. Draw one thing they might be pulling.

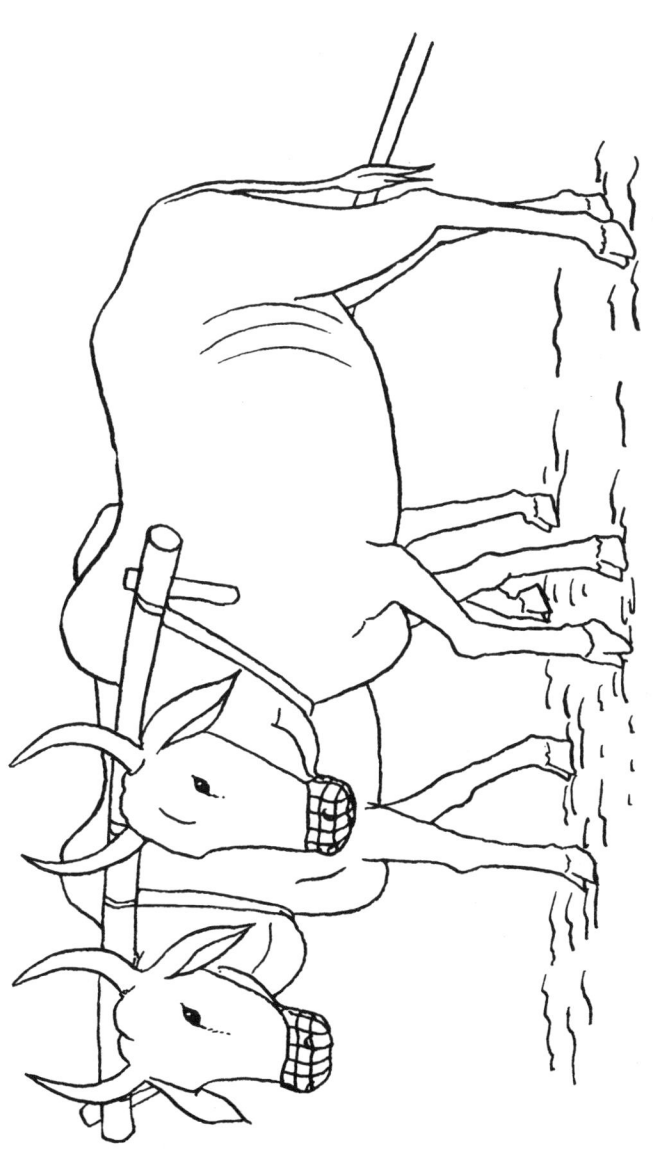

Can you name any other things the bulls might pull?

PROGRAMME 3

Anancy the Spider
A Caribbean Story

Learning outcomes

As a result of the programme children should have had experiences which enable them to:

- recognise that non-standard English plays an important part in our language heritage
- appreciate that spoken dialects of English from different parts of the world are at the heart of the oral tradition
- talk about some abstract ideas – for example greed, sharing, and wisdom – and help the children think about these
- recognise what a headline is and write headlines for a newspaper story
- find out about spiders and their habitats

Programme outline

The programme tells a story from Tobago about Anancy the Spider, who tried to collect and hide all the wisdom in the world. But he dropped and spilled it, and ran to hide in the corner, where he can be found to this day.

We are given a lot of information about spiders and some idea of the climate and environment of the Caribbean.

Key vocabulary

collect, habitat, spider, wisdom, greed, sharing, generous, lazy, tricky, tantalising, dialect

Before the programme

- Investigate small creatures, in particular spiders.
- Read a variety of Anancy stories and locate Tobago on a map.
- Read some 'rap' poems and introduce children to the idea of dialect. Collect some dialect words of the children's own and make a simple dialect dictionary.

Whilst watching

Ask the children to look out for animals and creatures which are different to those found in our country. Again note the direction in which we are flying and the physical features below. Pause the programme to make children aware of the dialect they hear.

Follow-up activities

▶ Find out all you can about spiders and record your findings in a class book. What do spiders prey upon, and what creatures prey upon them? The worksheet 'Number rhyme' could follow from this.

▶ Make Anancy from an egg-box and pipe-cleaners. Make a spider mobile.

▶ Collect some spiders and examine them under a microscope. Draw them. Be sure to return them to their environment.

▶ Look at some spiders' webs, especially on a dewy or frosty morning. Draw one. Do not break the web.

▶ Learn *Incy Wincy Spider*. Talk about rhyming words. Write a spider poem.

▶ Read *Caribbean Poems* by John Agard. Make a rap about Anancy. Have a class reading and pick your favourite.

▶ Talk about abstract ideas such as wisdom, greed, honesty and sharing. How can Anancy gather and store wisdom?

▶ Read *Not a Copper Penny in me House : Poems from the Caribbean* by Monica Gunning. How is the life of the people of Tobago different from ours?

▶ Anancy was the first news reporter in the Caribbean. Use the worksheet 'Spider spills the wisdom' to write a newspaper story about the event. Draw the children's attention to headlines and captions.

Spider spills the wisdom

Tobago Tatler

Local reporter, Anancy, missing

story by ....

ACTIVITY SHEET 5

Number rhyme

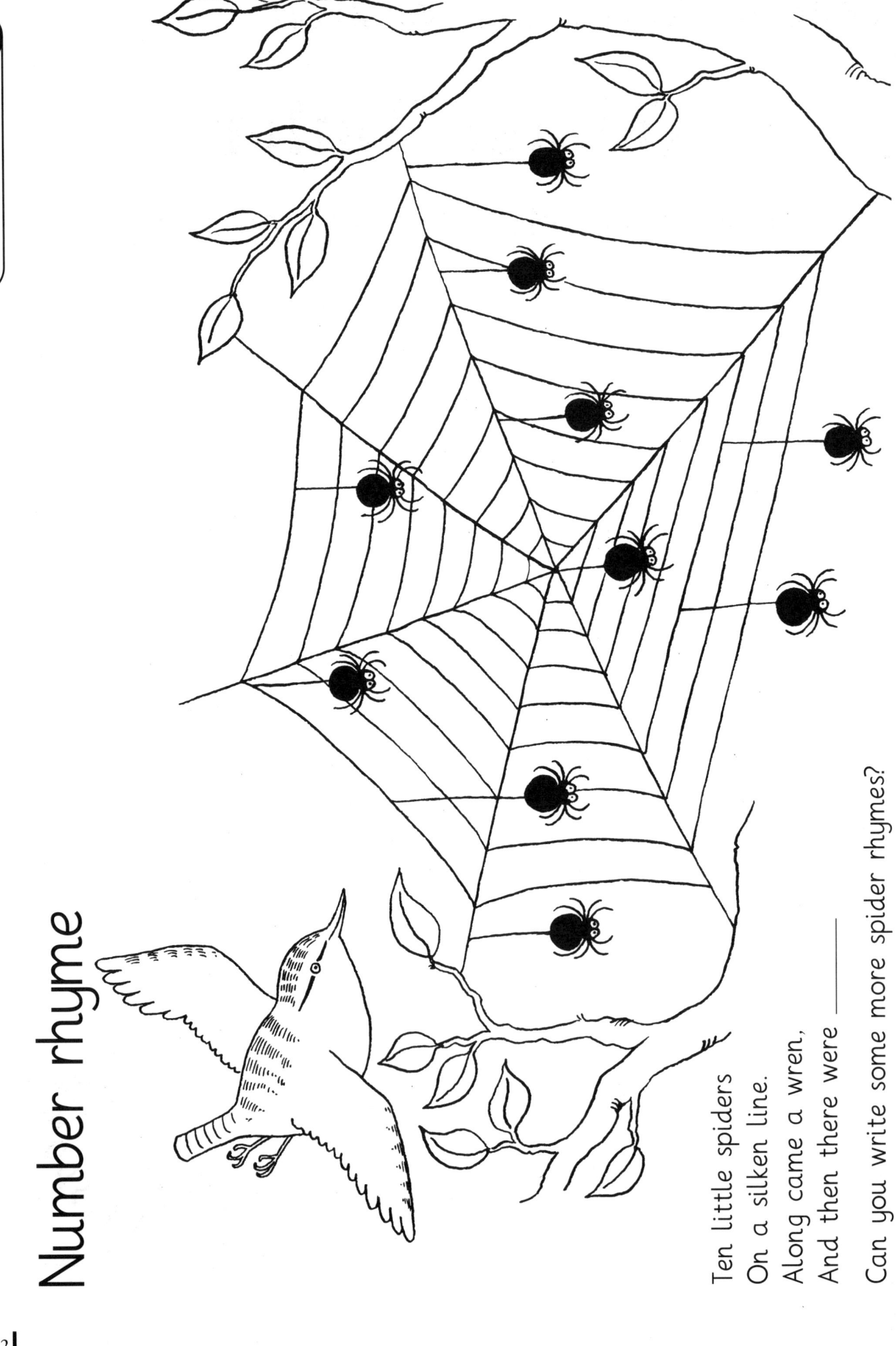

Ten little spiders
On a silken line.
Along came a wren,
And then there were ———

Can you write some more spider rhymes?

The Cat

An international story set in Ancient Egypt

Learning outcomes

As a result of the programme children should have had experiences which enable them to:

- explore different ways of retelling the international story
- recognise that some stories explain events in the history of man
- recognise the differences between wild and domestic animals
- understand that domestic animals need to be cared for and that this is a responsibility for anyone who keeps pets
- understand that man once lived in a more primitive way than we do today

Programme outline

This is an international story set in Egypt, home of the Sphinx storyteller. It tells how Cat followed Wild Dog, Cow and Horse to Man's dwelling and tricked Woman into giving her a place by the fire, although she is sure she will 'always be wild'. We learn that man tamed some animals for his own use.

This time the journey takes us south across the landscape of Britain and Europe to Africa and Egypt, where we see desert, cities, pyramids and the river Nile. We take a close look at wild cats and how they hunt, and we see how they resemble domestic cats.

Key vocabulary

primitive, wild, domestic, tame, pyramid, sphinx, landscape, families, dwellings

Before the programme

- Discuss how animals may first have been tamed.
- Talk about pets and how to care for them.
- Read some 'cat' poems.
- Look at pictures of wild cats.
- Locate Egypt on map of the world.
- Look at pictures of pyramids and sphinxes.

Whilst watching

Pause the programme and continue to draw attention to directions and landscape features. Ask children to note the variety of wild cats and other wild animals they see.

Follow-up activities

▶ Retell the story using shadow puppets. Make a puppet theatre using a cardboard box and an old sheet and a torch.

▶ Talk about pets and their needs: food, bedding, care, love and kindness.

▶ Record the number and variety of class pets on a graph or chart.

▶ Investigate animal homes and habitats: (i) wild animals and (ii) farm animals. Use the worksheet 'Friends and foes' to investigate wild and tame animals.

▶ Visit a working farm and talk to the farmer.

▶ Research wild cats and where they live.

▶ Trace the development of man's homes through the ages, starting from a simple cave dwelling.

▶ Read *How the Whale Became and Other Stories* by Ted Hughes. Discuss whether the stories are true or not.

▶ Provide books on Ancient Egypt and help the children research what life was like there. Why was the cat revered in Ancient Egypt? Find pictures of mummified cats to show to the children. Also look at cat and other animal masks. The children could make a mask.

▶ Look at the similarities between wild and domestic cats. Note how they are equipped for hunting. For example, observe their feet, claws, legs and teeth. You may use the cloze worksheet as a follow-up.

▶ Talk about what Cat might have said to persuade Woman to let him in. Work in pairs to create a dialogue for the worksheet 'Cat wants to sit by the fire'.

Cat wants to sit by the fire

Name_____

Write what they say to each other.

Friends and foes

Which of the animals are wild, and which are tame? Write 'W' or 'T' beside them.

Which eats which? Draw arrows from eater to eaten.

PROGRAMME 5

The Laidly Worm
An old English story

Learning outcomes

As a result of the programme children should have had experiences which enable them to:

- recognise the differences between a true story and a myth
- think about how stories are sometimes told in stained-glass windows
- learn some facts about slow-worms and hibernation
- understand that castles were built long ago when the landscape was different from today's

Programme outline

The story of the Laidly Worm is told through a stained-glass window of Durham Cathedral. The princess is changed into a slow-worm and then into a dragon by a jealous stepmother. The dragon is forced to obey the stepmother, and terrorises the Northumbrian countryside until the princess's brother returns from abroad. He recognises his sister inside the dragon form and he kisses her, breaking the spell. The stepmother is changed into a toad in retribution. The programme gives some facts about slow-worms and shows a landscape changing through the ages.

Key vocabulary

stained-glass, castle, knight, princess, hibernate, life cycle, reptile, terrorise, jealous

Before the programme

- Talk about slow-worms and animals that hibernate.
- Look at some pictures of medieval castles, knights and princesses.
- Look at some stained-glass church windows.
- Help children to think about directions.

Whilst watching

Remind the children to look for directions – north, south, east or west – and pause the programme on second viewing to observe how the story is told in stained-glass windows.

Follow-up activities

▶ Collect and tell some other myths and legends, and mark their country of origin on a world map.

▶ Talk about jealousy, and collect other stories that have the same theme, for example Snow White and The Children of Lir.

▶ Look at pictures of medieval knights and their armour or visit a castle or museum where some armour is on display.

▶ Research castles in your own locality and make a model of a castle with a moat, drawbridge and portcullis, using kitchen roll holders and other scrap materials.

▶ Make a pizza 'coat of arms' using cut-out pizza base, pizza dough and cheese slices cut into shapes.

▶ Introduce simple tapestry work, which dates from medieval times. Experiment with differently coloured wool to make interesting patterns.

▶ Find out about animals that hibernate, and make an information booklet.

▶ Research slow-worms, their habitats and life cycle.

▶ Investigate how and why stained-glass windows were made.

▶ Use the worksheet 'Make a stained-glass window' to make a jigsaw, sequence the story and make the stained-glass window by colouring it in.

▶ Use the template to make other stained-glass windows using tissue paper.

▶ Use the sorting worksheet 'Then and now' to provoke discussion about how people once lived. Children may stick the pictures in a book and add others of their own choosing.

Make a stained-glass window

Wren

Cut out the pieces carefully and make the jigsaw.
Stick onto light card and colour in the stained-glass window.

Then and now

Cut out the pictures and sort them into long ago and now.

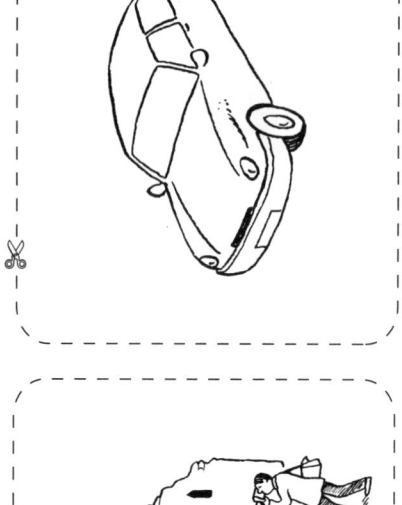
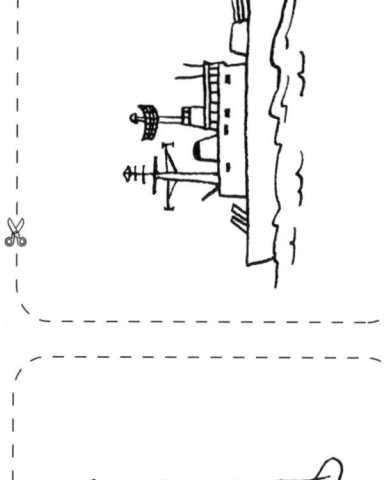

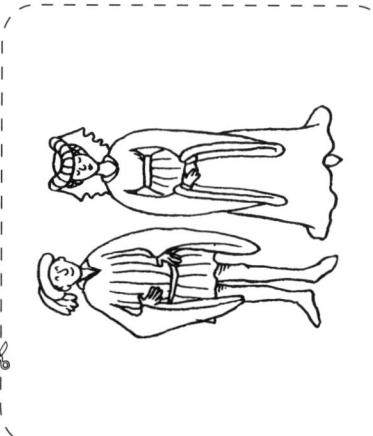
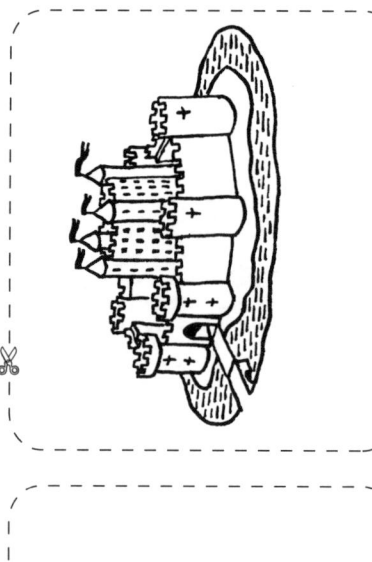

Can you find some more pictures of things from long ago and now?

What are the animals looking for?

Draw a line, then colour the paths.

| Cat | red | Laidly Worm | blue | Anancy | green | Wren | yellow | Biswas | brown |

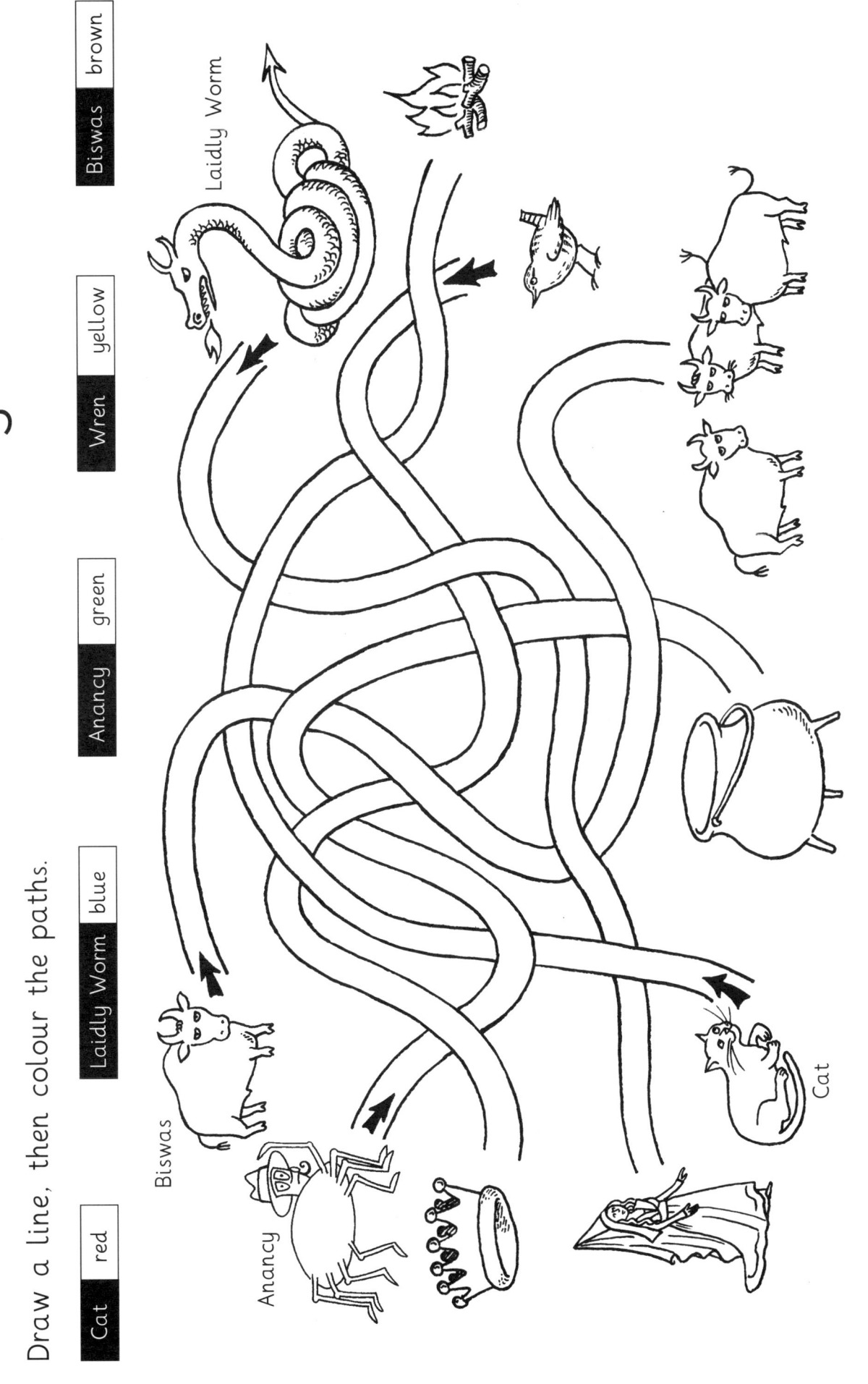

Riddle

Join the dots to find out who I am.

I am older than you can believe,
and wiser than you can understand,
I am half woman, half cat,
I tell stories about who you are
and where you come from.

I am a S_ _ _ _ _ _

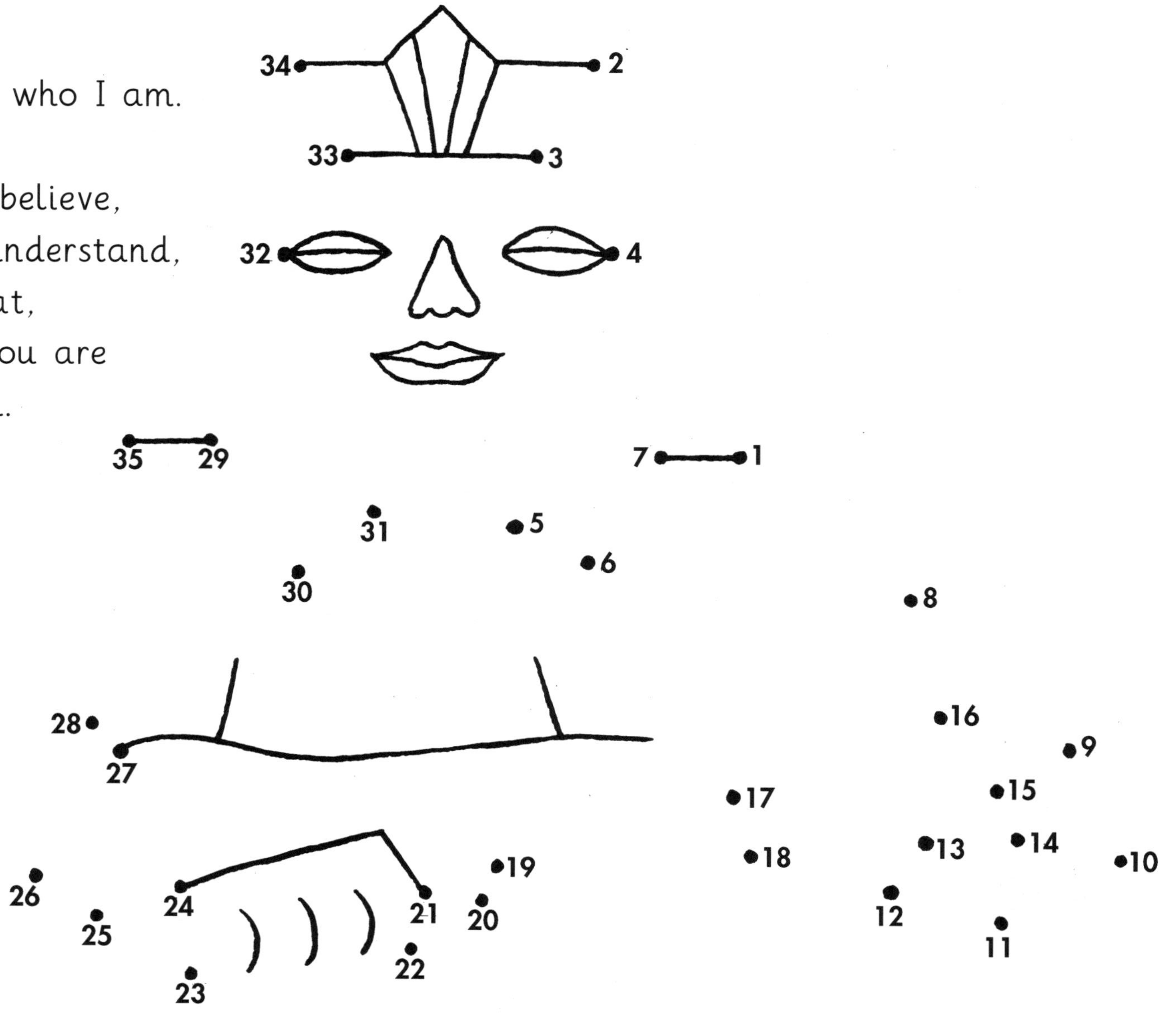

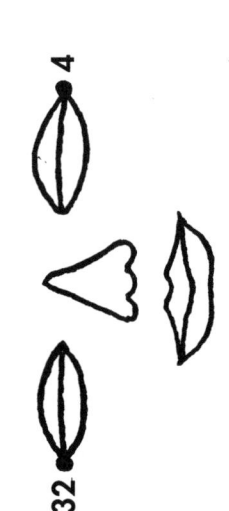